WHAT FAMILIES WERE LIKE

ANCIENT GREECE

ALISON COOPER

H O D D E R
Wayland

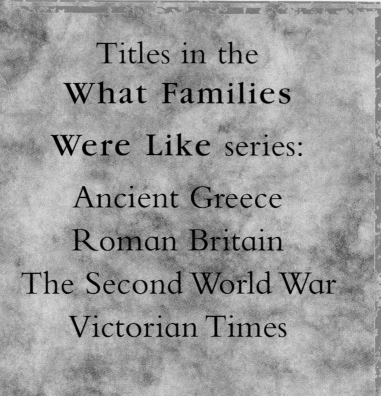

Titles in the
What Families

Were Like series:

Ancient Greece
Roman Britain
The Second World War
Victorian Times

This book is a simplified version of the title *Ancient Greece*
in Hodder Wayland's 'Family Life' series
Text copyright © 2001 Hodder Wayland
Volume copyright © 2001 Hodder Wayland

Language level consultant: Norah Granger
Editor: Belinda Hollyer
Designer: Jane Hawkins

First published in 2001 by Hodder Wayland, an imprint of Hodder Children's Books.

This paperback edition published in 2005

British Library Cataloguing in Publication Data
Cooper, Alison
What families were like - Ancient Greece
1.Family - Greece - History - Juvenile literature.
I.Title II. Ancient Greece
938
ISBN 0 7502 4734 7

Printed in China

Hodder Children's Books
A division of Hodder Headline Limited
338 Euston Rosd, London NW1 3BH

Picture acknowledgements:
Cover: head of Aphrodite Michael Holford, plate & terracotta figure G.M. Dixon;
Lesley and Roy Adkins 27 (top), 28 (top); Archiv für Kunst und Geschichte 23 (top)
British Museum; Bridgeman Art Library 15 Vatican Museums and Galleries, Rome;
C M Dixon 6 British Museum, 10 (left and right) both British Museum, 12 (top), 14
(top and bottom), 16 (top and bottom), 18, 21 National Museum, Athens, 24 (top)
National Museum, Athens; Robert Harding 4 British Museum; Michael Holford 7
(top and bottom) British Museum, 8 British Museum, 9 (left and right) both British
Museum, 11 British Museum, 12-13 (bottom) British Museum, 13 British Museum,
17, 19 British Museum, 20, 23 (bottom), 25 British Museum, 27 (bottom) British
Museum, 28 (bottom) British Museum; Zefa 22. Artwork: Nick Hawken 5, 8 (top),
24 (bottom); Peter Bull 26, 29.

CONTENTS

ANCIENT GREECE

Around 4,000 years ago Greece was made up of many small kingdoms. These kingdoms were powerful for about 1,000 years. Then there were wars and famines. People struggled to survive.

The city states

By 800 BC life had started to get better. Greece was now divided into city states instead of kingdoms. Each city state was made up of a city and the land and villages around it. Athens was the biggest.

In each city there was an area called the acropolis. It was usually the highest place in the city, so that it could be defended. The Ancient Greeks built a temple in the acropolis to honour a god or goddess.

▲ This vase was made between 800 and 500 BC. It shows a farmer harvesting olives.

At first all the city states except Sparta were governed by groups of noblemen. Later, other powerful men, such as merchants and craftsmen, began to demand a say in how the states were run. Trouble broke out again in Ancient Greece.

Tyrants

By about 650 BC the people had had enough of different groups fighting for control. They thought that it would be better to be ruled by one powerful man, who could keep everyone in order. These rulers were called tyrants.

This is a drawing of the Acropolis in Athens. People believed the goddess Athena looked after Athens. ▼

Main temple of Athena – the Parthenon

Gateway to the main temple area

Temple of Athena Nike, which means 'Athena, goddess of victory'

Statue showing Athena as a warrior and protector of the city.

Democracy

Eventually the Greeks decided that they did not want to be ruled by tyrants any longer. In 508 BC the people of Athens decided to govern their city in a new way. They held elections, and all the citizens voted for the men they wanted to run the city.

The new system was called democracy. Later other Greek city states copied the idea. Democracy did not mean that everyone could vote in the elections. Only citizens could take part. Women and slaves were not allowed to be citizens. Men who had been born outside the city state could not be citizens either.

▲ This plate shows a man hunting with his dog. The Greeks hunted for sport, as well as to catch animals for food.

Sparta

Sparta was different from the other Greek states. About 740–720 BC the Spartans had conquered their neighbours, the Messenians, but later on the Messenians had rebelled against them. After this, the Spartans tried to make sure that no one would ever dare to attack them again. All the Spartan men had to be soldiers. The most important job for the women was to produce sons who could become soldiers too.

▲ This is a statue of Pericles. The people of Athens elected him many times to be one of their leaders.

This is a Spartan girl athlete. Spartan girls did a lot of exercise to make them strong, so that they would have healthy children. ▶

LIFE AT HOME

This drawing shows what the home of a fairly rich family would have looked like. ▼

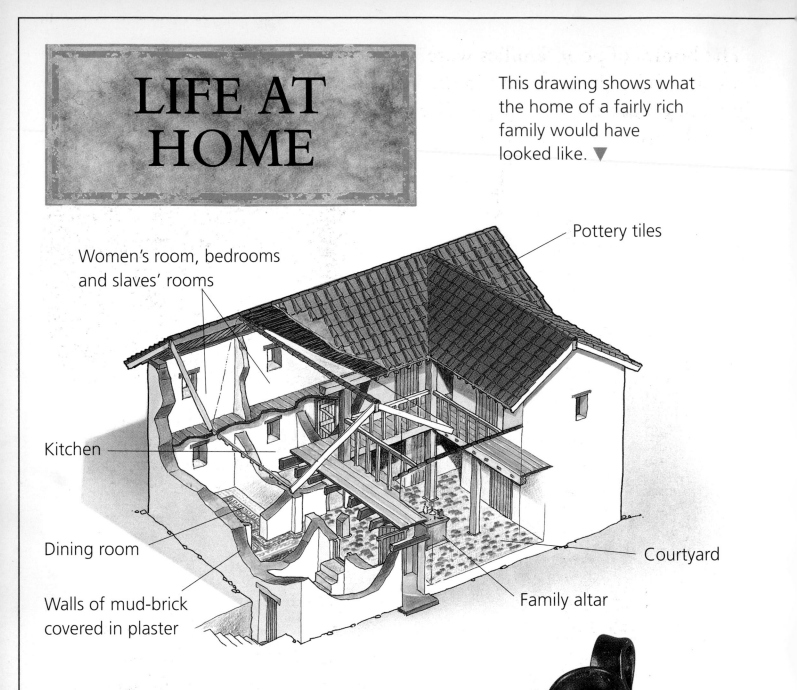

Pottery tiles

Women's room, bedrooms and slaves' rooms

Kitchen

Dining room

Walls of mud-brick covered in plaster

Courtyard

Family altar

Houses

Greek houses were usually built around a courtyard. In the courtyard there was an altar where the family worshipped the gods. Rich families had a well there too. Families who could not afford their own well had to fetch water from a public fountain.

▲ This is a baby's feeding bottle.

The homes of poor families were much smaller than the one in the picture on the opposite page. They lived in just one or two rooms.

▲ The picture on this vase shows a baby on a chair. There was a hole in the seat with a potty underneath it.

Childhood

When a baby was born it was shown to its father. If he was pleased with it, it was allowed to live. If he did not like it, or if it did not look very healthy, it was left outside to die.

When a baby was seven days old the family held a party and gave the baby gifts. When it was ten days old they gave it a name.

▲ Little girls played with dolls like this.

Boys

Poor boys did not go to school. Their fathers could not afford to pay for lessons. Richer boys started school when they were 7 years old. They learned maths, reading, writing, music and poetry.

▲ These girls are playing a game called knucklebones. It was very popular in Ancient Greece.

Dance and athletics were important lessons because they helped to make boys fit and strong. When they were eighteen, all boys had to learn how to be soldiers. Richer boys stayed at school until they were eighteen. Poorer boys worked for a few years before they did military training.

In Sparta, boys started training to be soldiers when they were just 7 years old. They had to leave home and live in barracks. They were treated harshly, because people thought this would make them brave fighters.

◀ Greek children had pets to play with, as well as toys.

Girls

Girls did not go to school. They learned how to look after a home instead. When a girl was about fifteen her father chose a husband for her. Girls usually had to marry men who were much older than them.

This picture shows a young bride getting ready for her wedding. ▼

Married life

When a girl got married she had to sacrifice all her toys. This showed that her childhood was over. She would not have time to play with toys any more.

◀ This model shows a woman preparing a meal.

A woman who married a rich man had slaves to do the housework for her. She made sure the slaves did their jobs properly. She also looked after the children and cared for anyone in the family who was ill.

A woman who married a poor man had to do all the cooking and cleaning herself. Poor families usually ate bread or porridge, with some fruit or vegetables. Sometimes they had fish, but they could only afford meat on very special occasions.

Another important job for a poor woman was weaving. She wove cloth to make sheets and towels, as well as clothes for her family.

Women spent nearly all their time at home. Poor women went out to do the shopping, but rich women only went out to visit their friends. Sometimes rich women were allowed to take part in a religious festival.

Only a woman from a rich family would have worn a fashionable gold necklace like this. ▶

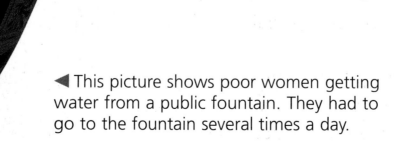

◀ This picture shows poor women getting water from a public fountain. They had to go to the fountain several times a day.

MEN'S LIVES

▲ This is a picture of Plato, a famous philosopher.

Greek men did not spend much time with their families. They were too busy working or helping to decide how the city state should be run. When they had some spare time they enjoyed a good dinner and a talk with other men. Spartan men lived in barracks for most of the time, even after they got married.

Philosophers

Philosophers were men who studied subjects such as maths, history and astronomy. They were a bit like teachers in a university. Young men often went to listen to them, and talk about their ideas. One of the most famous philosophers was called Plato. He set up a school called the Academy.

This is Socrates, a famous philosopher who lived from about 469 BC to 399 BC. ▶

Being good citizens

Many men spent some of their time helping to run their city state. In Athens, for example, all the citizens could take part in the Assembly. The Assembly voted for officials who made sure that everything in the city ran smoothly. It made other important decisions too, such as how to make sure there was enough food for everyone, or whether they should go to war with another state.

A Council of 500 men put forward ideas for the Assembly to discuss. Council members were not elected. They were picked at random, and served for just one year.

The Greeks told many stories about heroes from the past. This vase shows two of them, Ajax and Achilles. They are playing a board game. ▶

Earning a living

Men in Ancient Greece did not spend all their time voting or talking! There were many craftsmen who made fine pottery, jewellery and furniture. Most craftsmen had a paid worker and one or two slaves to help in the workshop.

In the countryside men worked hard on farms. They grew mainly grain, grapes and olives. The grapes were used to make wine and the olives were pressed to produce oil.

▲ This carving shows a carpenter sawing a plank of wood. Perhaps he is making a new chest, a seat or a table for a rich family.

This is a metalworker in his forge. He is holding a hammer and a pair of tongs. ▶

Wars

Greek citizens aged between 20 and 50 had to be ready to go and fight if war broke out. There were many wars between the city states. Life became very hard for the women and children if the man in the family was killed.

Sparta

Life in Sparta was very different from Athens. Even men who had been born in Sparta did not have much say in how their state was run. People who came from outside Sparta had no rights at all. Most of these people worked on farms. They had to give most of the food they produced to their Spartan masters. Spartan men had no time for farming – they were all soldiers.

▲ Soldiers wore helmets like this which protected their faces. This bronze helmet was captured by men from a state called Argos during a war against Corinth.

RELIGION

The Ancient Greeks worshipped twelve great gods and goddesses, as well as many other less important ones. They believed that these gods and goddesses looked after every part of their lives.

The king of the gods was called Zeus. His wife's name was Hera and she was the goddess of women and marriage. Athena was the goddess of war and wisdom. She also looked after the city of Athens. Hestia was the goddess of the home and family. Many Greek families showed their respect for Hestia by keeping a fire burning in a special room in their homes.

▲ This picture shows a woman making an offering at a family altar.

Family prayers

Religion was very important to families. They prayed to the gods at home every day. The father of the family led the prayers. Women made offerings at the family altar in the courtyard. Special events such as weddings always took place at home. But people did sometimes go to a temple to pray.

Temples

Every city in Ancient Greece had many beautiful temples. A different god or goddess was worshipped in each one. When a festival took place in honour of a god or goddess, a grand procession walked through the city to the temple.

This is part of a statue of Aphrodite. She was the goddess of love and beauty. ▶

The river of death

When a person died their body was buried or burned. The body or ashes were placed in a tomb. The Greeks believed that when they died their soul had to cross the river of death, which was called the River Styx. A ferryman called Charon would take them across in his boat, as long as their relatives remembered to put a coin in the tomb to pay him.

This is the ruined temple of Apollo at Delphi. Apollo was sometimes called the god of the sun. He was the god of music, poetry and medicine too.▼

Tombstones often showed the dead person with a member of their family. This man's tombstone shows him with his son.

The Underworld

When the souls of the dead had crossed the river, they entered the Underworld. A fierce dog with three heads guarded the entrance, in case any souls tried to escape. Souls were judged in the Underworld. Very good souls were sent to a beautiful place called the Elysian Fields. Very bad souls were sent to be punished for ever in Tartarus. Souls that were not very good but not especially bad went to the Asphodel Fields. This was a grey, boring place.

CITY LIFE

Greek cities were busy and noisy and the market was the busiest place of all. Shoppers crowded round the stalls, looking for the best vegetables and the freshest fish. They could buy many other goods here too – everything from a pair of sandals to a new slave. In rich families it was usually the men or the slaves who did the shopping.

▲ This is what the ancient marketplace in Athens looks like today. The Greek word for marketplace was *agora*.

If a shopper needed more money he could go to the banker's stall and borrow some. Each city had a different kind of money. Visitors had to swap their own coins for the coins used in the city.

The *stoa*

Around the marketplace there was a covered area called a *stoa*. Its roof was held up by columns.

▲ This Greek coin is made of silver.

This is the *stoa* around the main marketplace in Athens. It has been rebuilt to show what it looked like when it was new, just over 2,000 years ago. ▼

The *stoa* was a good place for people to meet and chat. The philosophers you read about on page 14 often talked to their students in the shade of the *stoa*.

Behind the *stoa* there were shops selling luxury goods such as silk or jewellery. There might also be a school, a doctor's surgery and a barber's shop.

23

◀ These actors are holding masks. Actors always wore masks during a performance.

The theatre

Plays were put on as part of the religious festivals. It did not cost much to see a play, so many people went along to the large open-air theatres.

This drawing shows what a Greek theatre looked like. ▼

Some action took place here in the *proskenion*.

This was the *skene*. The scenery hung from here.

This area was called the *orchestra*. Most of the action of the play took place here.

The audience sat on stone seats in the *theatron*.

24

Women were not allowed to act, so all the women's parts were played by men. A group of men called the chorus helped to tell the story by making comments about what was happening.

This vase was given to a winner at the Olympic Games. The picture on it shows boys riding in a horse-race. ▶

The games

Every city held athletics contests during religious festivals too. Some contests, such as the Olympic Games, were famous throughout Greece. The Olympic Games took place every four years. All wars had to stop at this time, so that people could travel safely to the games. Athletes could compete in running races, boxing, wrestling, horse-racing, chariot-racing and the pentathlon.

LIFE ABROAD

By about 800 BC the population of Greece was getting bigger very quickly. There was not enough land for everybody. Some families thought they would have a better life if they went to live in another country.

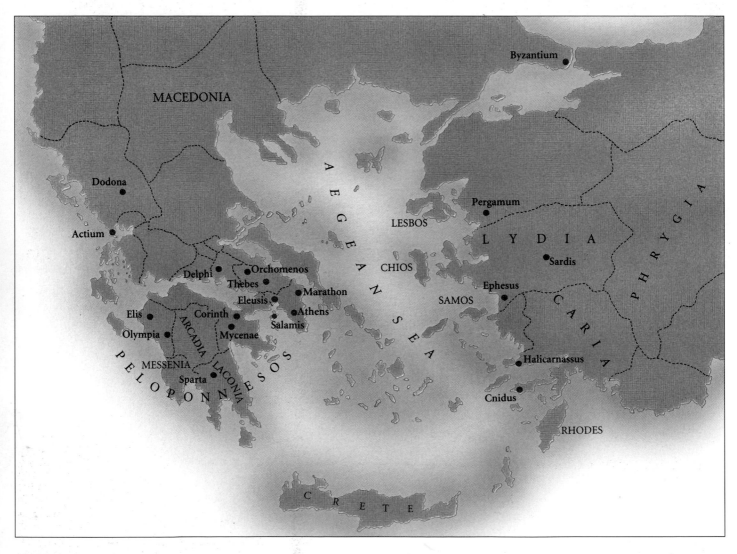

▲ This map shows the main cities of Greece and its colonies in Ionia.

Many Greek families went to live in Ionia. This was an area on the west coast of the country that we now call Turkey. Some went to live in the countries around the eastern Mediterranean Sea. Others went to southern Italy and France.

▲ Greek settlers worshipped Hera in this temple. The temple is in southern Italy.

The Greek settlers began to farm and build towns in their new lands. Ships loaded with goods sailed between Greece and the new colonies.

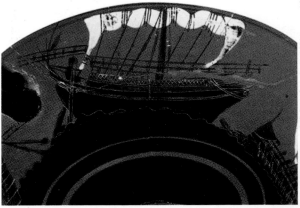

This is a picture of a trading ship. A warship is being rowed towards it and is going to ram it. ▶

This picture was made in Roman times. It shows Alexander the Great chasing away the Persian king. ▶

This bronze statue was found in a temple that Greek settlers built in north Africa. ▼

The Greeks and the Persians

The kings of Persia ruled an empire that stretched from the borders of India to the eastern coast of the Mediterranean Sea. Ionia was part of the Persian empire. In 499 BC the Greek settlers who lived there rebelled against the Persians. The Persian kings thought Greece was trying to take over their lands.

In 490 BC a Persian king called Darius invaded Greece, but his army was defeated. Ten years later a Persian king called Xerxes (pronounced 'Zerkzees') invaded Greece again. This time it looked as though the Persians would win. But the Greeks had a secret weapon – a huge fleet of fast warships called triremes. They used their ships to fight off the attack.

Alexander the Great

The Persians never attacked again but the Greeks and the Persians were always bitter enemies. In 334 BC a leader called Alexander led an army against the Persian empire. He conquered the Persians and became known as Alexander the Great. Now Greek ideas about art and science and the Greek way of life spread through the Middle East.

Later the Romans conquered the lands the Greeks had ruled. They took up some of the Greek ideas too. If you look back through this book, you will find some words and ideas that we still use even today.

This map shows the empire ruled by Alexander the Great. ▼

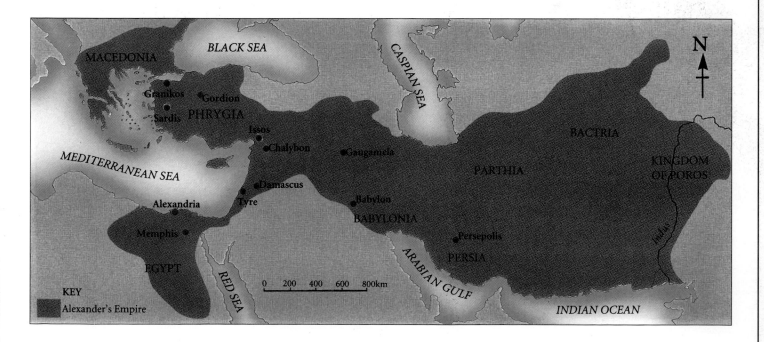

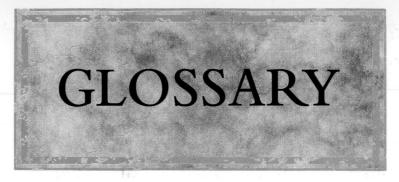

GLOSSARY

Altar A table where gifts are left for the gods, or animals are sacrificed.

Astronomy The study of stars and planets and how they move.

Athlete A person who takes part in sport.

Barracks A building where soldiers live.

BC This means 'Before Christ'. The year Jesus Christ was born is counted as the year 0. Years before this date are counted backwards, so 10 BC is ten years before Christ was born and 800 BC is 200 years further back in time than 600 BC.

Chariot A light wagon with two wheels, pulled by a horse. The driver rode in it standing up.

Colonies Areas in a country that are taken over by people from a different country.

Columns Tall stone or wooden posts that hold up a roof.

Election A contest between several people. The winner is the person or people who get the most votes.

Empire Many countries that are ruled by one king or emperor.

Famines Times when there is not enough food and people starve.

Forge A workshop where metal is beaten and shaped in a very hot fire.

Military training Learning how to be a soldier.

Offerings Gifts of food or money that people make to the gods.

Pentathlon A sports event made up of five activities. In Ancient Greece these were the long jump, discus, javelin, running and wrestling.

Persia A country in the Middle East. Today it is called Iran.

Rebelled Fought against their rulers.

Romans People who came from the city of Rome in Italy or other parts of the Roman Empire. The Romans conquered most of the lands around the Mediterranean Sea 2,000 years ago.

Sacrifice To kill or destroy something in order to please the gods.

Slaves People who were owned by other people. They had to work for their owner and they did not get paid.

Temple A place where a god or goddess was worshipped.

Books to read

Clothes of the Ancient World by Christine Hatt (Belitha, 2001)

History Starts Here: the Ancient Greeks by John Malam (Hodder Wayland, 2003)

Look Inside a Greek Theatre by Peter Chrisp (Hodder Wayland, 2002)

The Winner's Wreath by Martyn Oliver (Watts, 2000)

Women in Ancient Greece by Fiona Macdonald (Belitha, 1999)

You Wouldn't Want to be a Slave in Ancient Greece by Fiona MacDonald (Hodder Wayland, 2001)

Places to visit

Ashmolean Museum, Beaumont Street, Oxford, OX1 2PH.
A fine collection containing interesting Greek and Roman objects.

Birmingham City Museum, Chamberlain Square, Birmingham, B3 3DH.
A museum and gallery with a very good archaeology section, containing Greek objects.

British Museum, Great Russell Street, London WC1B 3DG.
The largest and finest collection of Greek objects in Britain.

Capesthorne Hall, Macclesfield, Cheshire SK11 9JY.
The house contains an important collection of Greek vases.

Fitzwilliam Museum, Trumpington Street, Cambridge CB2 1RB.
A museum which contains many fine ancient Greek works of art.

Greek Museum, University Department of Classics, Newcastle-upon-Tyne NE1 4XW.
This museum houses a fine collection of Athenian pottery, and a range of Greek weapons and armour.

If you visit Greece or the Greek islands on holiday, you will be able to visit the fine museums as well as the magnificent ruins. The south of Italy once had Greek colonies, and also has some important sites to visit.

INDEX